Helen T. Fou

# SALZBURG TRAVEL GUIDE UNVEILED 2024

## The Most Completed Pocket Guide to Discover Salzburg Hidden Treasure

## Table of Contents

# Introduction

Best regards and warm welcome to the charming city of Salzburg! This picturesque destination in the heart of Austria is known for its rich history, cultural heritage and breathtaking landscapes. As you embark on your journey through enchanting streets and picturesque landscapes, Salzburg promises a truly unforgettable experience that combines old world charm with modern delights.

Shrouded in architectural wonders, the city invites you to explore its cobblestone streets adorned with timeless structures that tell the stories of centuries past. The majestic Hohensalzburg Fortress watches over the city and offers panoramic views that will undoubtedly amaze you. Whether you're an art lover, history buff, or nature lover, Salzburg has something extraordinary to offer every visitor. As you navigate through this comprehensive travel guide, our goal is to serve as your trusted companion, providing valuable insights and practical advice to ensure your visit to Salzburg is nothing short of spectacular. We understand that every traveler is unique and seeks different experiences that resonate with their individual preferences.

This guide aims to cater to the diverse interests of our readers and offers a curated selection of attractions, activities and hidden gems that capture the true essence of Salzburg. From exploring the birthplace of Wolfgang Amadeus Mozart to enjoying the culinary delights of traditional Austrian cuisine, we have carefully crafted this guide to serve as your passport to an authentic and unforgettable experience in Salzburg.

As well as highlighting must-see sights and cultural treasures, we delve into the intricacies of local customs, giving you a deeper insight into the vibrant tapestry that is Salzburg. Whether you're a solo traveler, a couple looking for a romantic getaway, or a family looking for wholesome experiences, our guide is designed to meet your specific needs.

We recognize that travel is a personal journey and our goal is to give you the knowledge and confidence to explore Salzburg with ease. From practical travel tips to in-depth advice, consider this guide your gateway to discovering Salzburg's hidden wonders.

As you embark on this adventure, let the spirit of Salzburg guide you and every step will reveal a new aspect of this fascinating city. Prepare to immerse yourself in the magic of Salzburg, a destination where history, culture and natural beauty come together to create an experience that transcends time.

# History and Culture

A picturesque city located in the Austrian Alps, Salzburg has a rich history spanning more than 2,000 years. The name "Salzburg" means "salt castle" and reflects its historical significance as an important center for salt extraction and trade.

Salzburg's history dates back to the Roman Empire, when it was known as "Juvavum". The Romans recognized the strategic importance of the region thanks to its salt mines, which contributed to the city's early development.

Salzburg fell under Bavarian rule in the 8th century and became an ecclesiastical principality. The Archdiocese of Salzburg was founded and the city became an important center of Catholicism, influencing its cultural and architectural development. In the Middle Ages, famous monuments such as the Hohensalzburg Fortress were built, which stand proudly on the Festungsberg. The fortress remains one of the best preserved castles in Europe.

Perhaps Salzburg's most famous historical figure is Wolfgang Amadeus Mozart, born in the city in 1756. The house where he was born, now a museum, attracts music lovers from around the world.

The beginning of the 19th century brought with it the Napoleonic Wars which had an impact on the political landscape of Salzburg. The Congress of Vienna in 1814-1815 led to the creation of the

Austrian Empire and Salzburg became part of this influential empire.

Like many European cities, Salzburg also faced challenges during the two world wars. After World War II, the city was divided between the American and French zones of occupation. In 1955, Salzburg regained its status as part of the Republic of Austria.

Salzburg is synonymous with classical music, notably thanks to its most famous son, Wolfgang Amadeus Mozart. The city hosts the famous Salzburg Festival, a celebration of classical music and performing arts that attracts artists and audiences from around the world.

The cityscape is dominated by Baroque architecture, characterized by ornate facades and magnificent buildings. The UNESCO-listed Mirabell Palace and its gardens are an example of Salzburg's baroque splendor.

Salzburg's culinary scene combines traditional Austrian cuisine with international influences. Visitors can taste local specialties such as schnitzel, strudel and the famous Mozartkugel (Mozart chocolate). Salzburg's Christmas markets are world-famous and attract visitors with their festive atmosphere and wide range of handmade crafts, seasonal delicacies and traditional performances.

The city gained further fame thanks to the iconic film "The Sound of Music", which was filmed in and around Salzburg. Tourists often explore the film's locations, further contributing to the city's cultural identity.

In addition to the Salzburg Festival, the city hosts numerous cultural events, including the Salzburg Marionette Theatre, which celebrates the art of puppetry, and the Whitsun Festival, which offers a rich program of concerts and shows.

Salzburg's history is a tapestry woven from threads of salt trade, Roman influence, ecclesiastical power and musical genius. Deeply rooted in the past, its culture continues to flourish thanks to its architectural heritage, musical traditions and lively events that fascinate visitors from all over the world.

# Weather and Climate

Salzburg, Austria, has a humid continental climate (Köppen climate classification Dfb), with hot summers and cold, snowy winters. The city is located in the northern Limestone Alps, at an altitude of 431 meters above sea level. This elevation moderates the climate somewhat, making summers cooler and winters milder than at lower elevations.

Summers in Salzburg are warm and sunny, with average temperatures ranging from 18 to 25 degrees Celsius (64 to 77 degrees Fahrenheit). The warmest month is July, with an average temperature of 21.8 degrees Celsius (71.2 degrees Fahrenheit). Precipitation is relatively common in summer, with an average of 100 millimeters of precipitation per month. However, rain usually falls in short bursts and the sun shines for an average of 7 hours per day.

Winters in Salzburg are cold and snowy, with average temperatures of -2 to 3 degrees Celsius (28 to 37 degrees Fahrenheit). The coldest month is January with an average temperature of -0.7 degrees Celsius (30.6 degrees Fahrenheit). Snowfall is common in winter, with an average of 15 centimeters (6 inches) of snow on the ground at any time. In winter the city receives an average of 200 millimeters of precipitation per month, most of which falls as snow.

Spring and autumn are mild seasons in Salzburg, with temperatures ranging from 10 to 15 degrees Celsius (50 to 59 degrees Fahrenheit). Precipitation is common in both spring and autumn, averaging 90 millimeters of precipitation per month. However, in both seasons the sun shines for an average of 5 hours a day.

**Here you will find a table with average temperatures and precipitation for each month in Salzburg:**

| MONTH | AVERAGE Temperature (°C) | AVERAGE Precipitation (mm) |
|---|---|---|
| January | 0.7 | 79.2 |
| February | 0.6 | 84.5 |
| March | 4.0 | 75.7 |

| | | |
|---|---|---|
| **April** | 9.5 | 84.9 |
| **May** | 12.7 | 111.4 |
| **June** | 17.3 | 102.8 |
| **July** | 18.9 | 100.3 |
| **August** | 18.4 | 95.2 |
| **September** | 13.6 | 81.4 |
| **October** | 8.9 | 72.2 |
| **November** | 4.1 | 65.1 |
| **December** | 0.1 | 59.7 |

In general, Salzburg has a pleasant climate, with warm summers and mild winters. The city is a popular tourist destination all year round, and the weather is one of the reasons why.

# Best Time to Visit

**Best time to visit Salzburg**

Salzburg, Mozart's birthplace and a UNESCO World Heritage Site, is a beautiful city to visit all year round. However, the best time to visit Salzburg depends on your interests and preferences.

**September and October:** These are the most popular months to visit Salzburg, as the weather is pleasant and the crowds are fewer than in summer. The average temperature in September is 20°C and in October 14°C. The leaves begin to change color in October, creating a picturesque scene. May and June: These months are also good for a visit to Salzburg, as the weather gradually warms up and crowds are still relatively small. The average temperature in May is 61°F (16°C) and in June it is 70°F (21°C).

**Summer (July and August):** This is peak tourist season in Salzburg, so expect larger crowds and higher prices. However, the weather is also at its best during this time, with temperatures averaging between 20 and 30 degrees Celsius. Many festivals and events also take place in summer, such as the **Salzburg Festival. Winter (December and February):** Salzburg is a magical place to visit in winter with its Christmas markets, snow-covered hills and festive atmosphere. The average temperature in December is 32°F (0°C) and in February it is 37°F (3°C). Keep in mind, however, that some city attractions may be closed in winter.

**Salzburg Festival:** This is the oldest classical music festival in the world and takes place every summer from July to August.

**Christmas Markets:** Salzburg's Christmas markets are among the most famous in the world and are open from late November to December. Mozart Week: This festival takes place every January and celebrates the life and work of Wolfgang Amadeus Mozart.

**Easter Festival:** This festival takes place every spring and features classical music, theater and dance performances.

Whenever you decide to visit Salzburg, you are sure to have an unforgettable experience. This beautiful city has something to offer everyone, from its stunning architecture and rich history to its lively festivals and delicious food.

# Budgeting Tips

- Choose the right time to travel.

- Stay in a hostel or Airbnb.

- Use public transportation.

- Visit free attractions.

- Eat at local markets and cafes.

- Take advantage of student discounts.

- Cook your own meals.

- Pack your own snacks and drinks.

- Walk or bike around the city.

- Take advantage of free events

# Getting Acquainted with

# Salzburg

Often called the "city of Mozart" and "the Rome of the north", Salzburg is a charming and picturesque city in the heart of Austria. This UNESCO World Heritage Site is known for its rich history, stunning architecture and breathtaking Alpine setting. Salzburg is the capital of the state of Salzburg and is located on the banks of the Salzach River, with the Eastern Alps as a beautiful backdrop.

The history of the city dates back to Roman times, but its period of greatest flourishing was during the Middle Ages, when it became an important center for salt extraction. Hence the name: "Salzburg" means "Salt Fort". Situated atop the Festungsberg,

Hohensalzburg Fortress is a testament to the city's medieval past.

Salzburg is perhaps best known as the birthplace of Wolfgang Amadeus Mozart, one of history's greatest composers. Visitors can explore Mozart's birthplace and residence and delve into the life and work of this musical genius. The city's Baroque architecture, including Salzburg Cathedral and Mirabell Palace, further contributes to its cultural and historical significance.

Salzburg perfectly combines its historical roots with a vibrant contemporary culture. The Old Town (Altstadt) is a labyrinth of narrow streets and medieval squares, where you will find countless shops, cafés and restaurants. Stroll through Getreidegasse, a lively shopping street where you'll find Mozart's birthplace, as well as charming boutiques and traditional crafts.

Salzburg is a center for classical music, where the famous Salzburg Festival is held every summer. The city resonates with the melodies of Mozart and visitors can attend concerts at venues such as the Mozarteum and the Salzburg Marionette Theatre. "The Sound of Music," a classic film set in the breathtaking landscape of Salzburg, has also left an indelible mark on the city's cultural identity.

Nature lovers can explore the surrounding Salzkammergut, known for its untouched lakes and alpine landscapes. The neighboring Untersberg offers panoramic views of the city and the Austrian countryside.

By immersing yourself in Salzburg's unique culture, respecting local customs and exploring its historical and artistic treasures, you are sure to have an unforgettable and enriching travel experience in this fascinating Austrian city.

# Navigating the City

Consider the Salzburg Card for an all-in-one solution. This pass offers unlimited access to public transport, including buses and trams, and free entry to many museums and attractions. It's a convenient way to explore the city while enjoying its cultural offerings.

### 4.1.3 Buses

Salzburg's bus network completely covers the city and its suburbs. The buses are punctual, clean and a great way to get to various attractions. Tourists can get route maps from information centers or use mobile apps for real-time updates.

### 4.1.4 Tram

Trams are another popular means of transport in Salzburg and connect important points of the city. They provide a beautiful ride and are a convenient way to get to destinations quickly.

### 4.1.5 Taxis and ride sharing

Taxis are available throughout the city and are a convenient alternative for those looking for door-to-door service. Additionally, ride-sharing apps operate in Salzburg, providing another flexible transportation option. 4.2 Walking excursions

### 4.2.1 Exploration of the historic center

The best way to explore Salzburg's historic center, a UNESCO World Heritage Site, is on foot. Walking tours allow tourists to enjoy the city's medieval charm, stroll along Getreidegasse with its boutiques and visit emblematic sights such as Mozart's birthplace and Hohensalzburg Fortress.

## 4.2.2 Tour All the sounds of music

For fans of the famous musical, a guided walking tour of the Sound of Music is a must. This tour takes visitors to film locations including Mirabell Gardens, Nonnberg Abbey and the von Trapp family home, providing a delightful experience for film buffs.

## 4.2.3 Self-guided tours

For a more personalized experience, self-guided walking tours allow tourists to explore the city at their own pace using maps or mobile apps.

Highlights often include Mirabell Palace, St. Peter's Abbey, and Salzburg Cathedral.

## 4.3 Cycle paths in Salzburg

### 4.3.1 Salzach cycle path

Cycling enthusiasts will appreciate the Salzach River Cycle Path, which offers a scenic route along the riverbanks. This trail offers great views of the cityscape and surrounding Alps, making it a favorite among locals and tourists alike.

### 4.3.2 Hellbrunn Castle Cycle Route

For a relaxing ride, the cycle path up to Hellbrunn Castle is ideal. This route takes cyclists through the outskirts of the city, past lush greenery and lovely palace gardens. 4.3.3 Bicycle rental

Several bicycle rental companies in Salzburg offer a wide range of bicycles for tourists. Renting a bike gives you the freedom to explore the outskirts of the city and explore the surrounding countryside.

With its blend of history and natural beauty, Salzburg is a city best explored using various means of transportation. Whether exploring the city on foot, embarking on a cycling adventure, or using public transportation, tourists are sure to discover the enchanting charm of this Austrian gem.

# The Heart of Salzburg: Old Town

## Residenzplatz and Residenzgalerie

Residenzplatz is the large central square in the heart of Salzburg's Old Town. Surrounded by historic buildings and architectural marvels, this bustling square is a hub of activity and a prime spot for visitors who want to immerse themselves in the city's rich culture. In the middle of Residenzplatz stands the magnificent Residenzbrunnen, a baroque fountain adorned with statues and reliefs that provides a picturesque focal point.

Next to Residenzplatz is the Residenzgalerie, an art gallery located in the Salzburg Residence, the former archbishops' palace. The Residenzgalerie has an impressive collection of European art from the 16th to 19th centuries, with works by renowned artists such as Rembrandt, Rubens and Brueghel. Tourists can explore the opulent rooms of the Residenz appreciating the masterpieces that adorn the walls and offer a unique blend of history and art.

**Salzburg Cathedral**

Salzburg Cathedral, also known as Salzburg Cathedral, is a masterpiece of Baroque architecture and a symbol of the city's religious heritage. The cathedral's magnificent façade and impressive dome dominate the Old Town skyline. Inside, visitors can marvel at the intricate details of the interior, including the impressive Baroque altar and the breathtaking frescoes on the ceilings. The cathedral also houses the crypt of Saint Rupert, the city's patron saint, giving this religious monument historical importance.

**Hohensalzburg Fortress**

The Hohensalzburg Fortress sits on the Festungsberg and is a landmark of Salzburg and one of the largest medieval castles in Europe. Accessible by funicular or via a steep but rewarding climb, the fortress offers panoramic views of the city and the surrounding Alps. Within its walls, visitors can explore the various courtyards, rooms and museums and thus immerse themselves in the medieval history of Salzburg. The fortress museum offers an insight into the construction of the castle and the daily life of its inhabitants.

# The Sound of Music Tour

**Mirabell Gardens**

Located in the heart of Salzburg, Austria, the Mirabell Gardens are a breathtaking horticultural masterpiece that perfectly combines natural beauty and historical significance. Known for its baroque design and meticulously landscaped landscapes, this iconic attraction has become a must-see destination for tourists seeking tranquility and cultural richness.

The Mirabell Gardens are conveniently located in the heart of Salzburg, adjacent to the Mirabell Palace. Its central location makes it easily reachable on foot and well connected to the city's public transport. Tourists can enjoy a pleasant walk in the historic center or hop on a local bus to reach this enchanting oasis. The Mirabell Gardens were originally designed in 1690 by Johann Bernhard Fischer von Erlach for Prince Archbishop Johann Ernst von Thun and have a rich history. The gardens were completely renovated under the direction of Franz Anton Danreiter, then embellished around 1730 by the famous architect Dominique Girard. The gardens and adjacent Mirabell Palace have witnessed cultural events for centuries and are now considered a UNESCO World Heritage Site.

**Main attractions:**

Pegasus Fountain: The Pegasus Fountain, a masterpiece by Kaspar Gras, dominates the central axis of the Mirabell gardens. The fountain represents the mythical winged horse Pegasus surrounded by four statues representing the four elements earth, fire, water and air. Hedge Theater: One of the unique features of Mirabell Gardens is the Hedge Theater, an open-air stage surrounded by greenery. This intimate setting is often used for concerts and shows, offering visitors a cultural treat amid the beauty of nature.

**Rose Garden**: The scent of blooming roses welcomes visitors to the Rose Garden, a carefully landscaped space with a diverse collection of roses. The vibrant colors and enchanting scents make it a popular spot for a leisurely stroll or romantic retreat.

**Orangery:** The Orangery is an elegant building located within the garden, initially intended for the cultivation of exotic plants. Today, various events take place there and serve as a picturesque backdrop for weddings and celebrations.

**Grand Parterre:** A pattern of carefully arranged flower beds, the Grand Parterre offers a visual spectacle with its geometric patterns. This area demonstrates the Baroque style and offers fantastic photography opportunities.

The Mirabell Gardens are not just a static attraction; It is a lively place where many events take place throughout the year. From classical music concerts to open-air theater performances, visitors have the opportunity to immerse themselves in the cultural diversity of Salzburg while enjoying the beauty of the gardens. Mirabell Gardens are generally open to the public all year round. However, it is advisable to check for any special events or maintenance closures before planning your visit. Entrance to the gardens is free, making it a destination accessible to everyone. Some garden events and attractions may have separate entrance fees. To better understand the history and significance of Mirabell Gardens, you should take a guided tour. Knowledgeable guides provide fascinating anecdotes and historical context to enhance your experience. The gardens offer wonderful photography opportunities, so don't forget your camera. Capture the intricate details of the sculptures, the vibrant colors of the flowers and the overall charm of this enchanting space.

The Mirabell Gardens in Salzburg are a sensory delight that combines the elegance of baroque design with the charm of carefully tended greenery. Whether you are a history buff, a nature lover or someone looking for cultural experiences, Mirabell Gardens is a destination that promises to leave an indelible mark on your Salzburg travel itinerary. Immerse yourself in the charm of this timeless masterpiece and let the beauty of the Mirabell Gardens create lasting memories of your visit to this picturesque Austrian city.

**Nonnberg Abbey**

Located in the heart of Salzburg, Austria, Nonnberg Monastery is a testament to centuries of history, spirituality and architectural splendor. As one of the oldest monasteries in German-speaking countries, Nonnberg Abbey offers a unique and enriching experience for tourists wishing to explore Salzburg's rich cultural heritage. Here's a comprehensive guide to help you get the most out of your visit to Nonnberg Monastery.

The Nonnberg Monastery, founded in 714, was built before the city of Salzburg. It has a rich history linked to the roots of Christianity in the region. The abbey is known as the home of Maria von Trapp, whose life story inspired the beloved musical "The Sound of Music." Its medieval architecture and picturesque surroundings make it a fascinating destination for history buffs. Nonnberg Abbey has been a place of worship and spiritual retreat for more than a millennium. The abbey is still active and the Benedictine nuns continue their religious practices. Visitors are invited to participate in the liturgical services, which offer a unique opportunity to witness the harmonious fusion of history and spirituality.

The architecture of the abbey is a mix of Romanesque and Baroque styles. The church, with its impressive interior and ornate details, is the highlight of the tour. The 12th century cloister is another architectural gem and offers a calm and contemplative atmosphere.

Nonnberg Abbey is generally open to visitors. Be sure to check the exact opening hours before planning your visit, however, as they are subject to change. Experienced guides lead tours of the abbey and provide insight into the history, architecture and daily life of the monastery. Visits are strongly recommended to fully understand the importance of the abbey. As Nonnberg Abbey is a religious site, visitors are advised to dress modestly. It is respectful to cover shoulders and knees and hats are generally not allowed in church.

Nonnberg Abbey has gained international fame due to its association with "The Sound of Music". Although the interior of the abbey was not used in the film, the courtyard served as the backdrop for some iconic scenes. Fans of the film can relive the magic by exploring this historic location. Nonnberg Abbey is conveniently located close to the heart of Salzburg and is easily accessible on foot or by public transport. Visitors can take a pleasant stroll through the charming streets of Salzburg to reach the abbey. Near Nonnberg Monastery, take the opportunity to explore other Salzburg attractions such as Hohensalzburg Fortress and Mirabell

Palace. The historic center of Salzburg, a UNESCO World Heritage Site, is a treasure trove of cultural and architectural wonders.

Nonnberg Abbey in Salzburg offers a captivating journey through time, spirituality and culture. Whether you're drawn to the historical significance, architectural beauty, or connection to "The Sound of Music," a visit to Nonnberg Abbey is an enriching experience that will give you a deeper understanding of Salzburg culture. So don't miss the chance to immerse yourself in the tranquility and history this venerable abbey has to offer.

# Exploring Mozart's Legacy

Wolfgang Amadeus Mozart, one of the most influential composers in the history of classical music, left an indelible mark on the world with his timeless compositions. Salzburg, Austria is the birthplace of Mozart's genius and therefore a place of pilgrimage for music lovers and tourists. This comprehensive guide will introduce you to the most important places associated with Mozart's life and legacy, ensuring an enriching and harmonious experience during your visit.

Start your trip with a visit to the house where Mozart was born on January 27, 1756. Located at 9 Getreidegasse in Salzburg, Mozart's Birthplace is a well-preserved museum that showcases the composer's early life, his family artifacts and rooms

46

where he spent his formative years. Visitors can explore displays of original instruments, portraits and personal items, providing an intimate insight into Mozart's education and 18th-century cultural context.

Next, head to Mozart's home, a short walk from his hometown, Makartplatz 8. This elegant mansion, where Mozart lived from 1773 to 1780, offers a glimpse into his adult life. The carefully restored rooms feature antique furniture, family portraits, and interactive exhibits highlighting Mozart's productive years in Salzburg. Concerts are also held at the residence, allowing visitors to experience Mozart's music where he once lived and composed.

Immerse yourself in Salzburg's vibrant musical culture by attending one of its renowned music festivals. The Salzburg Festival, held annually from late July to early September, is a highlight. Founded in 1920, the festival celebrates classical music, opera and theatre, often presenting performances of Mozart's masterpieces in historic venues such as Salzburg Cathedral and the Mozarteum.

Additionally, Mozart Week, which takes place in late January around the composer's birthday, honors Mozart's legacy with a series of concerts, operas and events. The variety of performances allows visitors to experience Mozart's music in various forms, from symphonies to operas to chamber music.

Exploring Mozart's legacy in Salzburg is a captivating journey that combines historical immersion, musical appreciation and the enchanting ambiance of this charming Austrian city. Whether you're an avid Mozart fan or a curious traveler, Salzburg offers a harmonious blend of cultural experiences that will leave a lasting impression.

# Culinary Delights in Salzburg

## Traditional Austrian Cuisine

The city's traditional Austrian cuisine reflects a harmonious blend of flavors influenced by the region's history and geography. In this Salzburg travel guide, we invite you on a gastronomic adventure to discover 10 traditional Austrian dishes that you absolutely must try in the charming city of Salzburg.

### 1. Wiener schnitzel:

Start your culinary journey with the iconic Wiener Schnitzel, a thinly pounded and breaded veal or pork cutlet. Served with a slice of lemon, this crunchy and tender dish is an indispensable part of Austrian cuisine.

## 2. Salzburger Nockerl:

Indulge your sweet tooth with Salzburger Nockerl, a delicious and airy soufflé dessert from Salzburg. Often served with powdered sugar and raspberry sauce, it's a treat for any sweet tooth.

## 3. Cheese dumplings:

For a tasty appetizer, try Kaspressknödel, cheese balls usually made from leftover bread and cheese. These hearty delights are often accompanied by a flavorful broth, creating a comforting and traditional Austrian dish.

## 4. Tafelspitz:

Tafelspitz, a classic Austrian beef dish, consists of Tafelspitz served with horseradish and various side dishes such as apple and chive sauce. Enjoy the tenderness of the meat and the variety of flavors that accompany it.

## 5. Brettljause:

Best Austrian sausages: Brettljause is a platter with a selection of sausages, cheese and pickles. This traditional dish is perfect for sharing and is often enjoyed with a glass of Austrian wine.

## 6. Dumplings:

A versatile Austrian staple, dumplings are dumplings that can be sweet or savory. Whether accompanied by potatoes, breadcrumbs or semolina, these dumplings come in a variety of shapes and are often served with strong sauces or fruit compotes.

## 7. Leberkäse:

Leberkäse, despite its name ("liver cheese" in German), actually contains no liver or cheese. This is a flavorful meatloaf made with finely ground corned beef, pork and bacon. Served hot, it represents satisfying and quick street food.

## 8. Apple strudel:

No Austrian culinary trip is complete without apple strudel, a delicious apple pie. Thin layers of dough envelop a blend of apples, sugar and spices, creating a dessert that perfectly captures the essence of Austrian comfort food.

## 9. Goulashsuppe:

Warm and hearty: Gulaschsuppe is a traditional Austrian goulash soup. This dish, made with tender meat, onions and peppers, showcases the rich flavors of Central European cuisine. It's the perfect choice for a hearty meal during the colder months.

## 10. Mozartkugel:

End your culinary exploration with a treat named after Salzburg's most famous son, Wolfgang Amadeus Mozart. Mozartkugel is a chocolate-coated almond paste nougat confection, a delicious souvenir to take home or enjoy while exploring the city.

Salzburg, with its rich history and cultural richness, offers not only visual and acoustic delights, but also a range of traditional Austrian dishes to delight the palate. Immerse yourself in Salzburg's culinary heritage and let these 10 delicious offerings form the centerpiece of your gastronomic adventure in this enchanting Austrian city.

## Popular Local Restaurants

When you visit Salzburg, be sure to explore these 10 popular local restaurants that offer a delicious dining experience.

### St. Peter Stiftskeller

*Location: St. Peter Bezirk 1/4, 5020 Salzburg*

The St. Peter Stiftskeller is one of the oldest restaurants in Europe and dates back to the 9th century. Nestled in the heart of the old town, it offers a historic ambiance and a varied menu with traditional Austrian dishes such as Wiener Schnitzel and hearty stews.

## Zum fidelen Affen

*Location: Judengasse 15, 5020 Salzburg*

Zum fidelen Affen, translated as "The Happy Monkey", is a charming restaurant with a cozy atmosphere. The menu includes Austrian specialties such as Tafelspitz and Kasnocken, known for their regional ingredients.

## Goldener Hirsch Restaurant

*Location: Getreidegasse 37, 5020 Salzburg*

The Goldener Hirsch restaurant is located in the famous Getreidegasse and is part of the legendary Goldener Hirsch Hotel. This upscale restaurant combines Austrian flavors with a modern touch. In an elegant ambiance, you can enjoy dishes such as roast venison and apple strudel.

**M32**

*Location: Mönchsberg 32, 5020 Salzburg*

For panoramic city views and culinary delights, head to the M32. This modern restaurant in Mönchsberg offers a varied menu with international influences. Try their creative dishes and don't miss the opportunity to dine on the terrace overlooking Salzburg.

## Triangel

*Location: Linzergasse 37, 5020 Salzburg*

Triangel is a hidden gem in the Linzergasse district. It has a relaxed atmosphere and serves traditional Austrian dishes. The menu includes classics like Goulash and Kaiserschmarrn, a fluffy shredded pancake.

## Agostino Brau

*Location: Lindhofstraße 7, 5020 Salzburg*

This renowned beer hall, part of the Augustinus brewery, is a favorite among locals and tourists alike. Augustiner Bräu offers a unique self-service experience where you can grab a tray, choose from a variety of Austrian dishes at different stands and enjoy a freshly brewed beer in a lively atmosphere.

**Bärenwirt**

*Location: Müllner Hauptstraße 8, 5020 Salzburg*

The Bärenwirt in the Mülln district is a traditional Austrian inn with rustic charm. Famous for its hearty portions, dishes like roast pork and ravioli are on the menu. The beer garden is perfect for enjoying the local ambiance.

**La Weisse**

*Location: Rupertgasse 10, 5020 Salzburg*

La Weisse, a historic brewery, is known for its selection of house-brewed beers and hearty Austrian cuisine. The beer garden and warm interior design guarantee an authentic experience. Be sure to try the pretzels and sausages.

## PitterKeller

*Location: Rainerstraße 6, 5020 Salzburg*

The PitterKeller is located in the heart of Salzburg and is an underground beer cellar with a lively atmosphere. This is the perfect place to enjoy traditional Austrian dishes such as roast pork and sample a variety of local beers.

## K+K Restaurant on Waagplatz

*Location: Waagplatz 2, 5020 Salzburg*

Located in a historic building overlooking Waagplatz, the K+K restaurant offers a mix of Austrian and international flavors. The menu features dishes prepared with local ingredients, ensuring a fresh and authentic dining experience.

Exploring Salzburg's culinary scene is an integral part of your trip, and these local restaurants promise to offer a true taste of Austrian hospitality and gastronomy. Enjoy your meal!

## Street Food Gems

However, no visit to Salzburg is complete without enjoying its diverse and delicious street food offering. From traditional Austrian delicacies to international flavours, Salzburg's street food scene is a culinary adventure waiting to be explored. Here are 10 street food gems that every tourist should know when visiting Salzburg.

**1. Bosna stand in Getreidegasse:**

Speciality: A must try is the Bosna, a grilled bratwurst sausage served on a bun with a unique blend of curry and onions.

**Location:** Find this iconic stand on Getreidegasse, one of Salzburg's most charming streets. Langos at

2. **Mirabellplatz market:**

**Speciality:** Langos, a Hungarian delight, is a fried flatbread topped with garlic, sour cream and cheese.

**Location:** Head to Mirabellplatz Market for an authentic Langos experience.

### 3. Käsekrainer of the Würstelstand am Franz-Josefs-Kai:

**Specialty:** A cheese-filled sausage, Käsekrainer, is grilled to perfection and often served with mustard.

**Location:** Visit the Würstelstand am Franz-Josefs-Kai for this tasty treat.

### 4. Mozartkugel ice cream at Eisdiele am Alter Markt:

**Speciality:** This ice cream is a creative twist on the famous chocolate Mozartkugel and has flavors of marzipan, nougat and pistachio. Location: Enjoy this sweet treat in the Alter Markt ice cream parlor.

## 5. Brettljause in the Augustiner Bräustübl:

**Speciality:** Discover the Austrian Brettljause with various cold meats, cheeses and freshly baked bread.

**Location:** Visit the Augustiner Bräustübl brewery for an authentic Brettljause experience.

## 6. Kaiserschmarrn at St. Gilgener Markt:

**Specialty**: Kaiserschmarrn is a sweet and fluffy grated pancake that is often served with powdered sugar and fruit compote.

**Location:** Find this delicious treat at the St. Gilgen market. Falafel Wrap at Afro Cafe:

**Speciality:** For a taste of international cuisine, try the falafel wrap at Afro Cafe, with tasty chickpea patties and fresh vegetables.

**Location:** Located in the heart of Salzburg, Afro Cafe offers a delicious alternative to Austrian cuisine.

## 7. Steckerlfisch at the Fischküche am Leopoldskroner Weiher:

**Speciality:** Grilled fish on a stick, or Steckerlfisch, is a popular lakeside snack, offering a delicious blend of smoky and savory flavors.

**Location:** Head to Fischküche am Leopoldskroner Weiher for a unique lakeside dining experience.

## 8. Pretzel at the Alter Markt:

**Speciality:** Taste the classic Austrian pretzel, or Bretzel, with its golden crust and soft interior.
**Location**: Many stalls around the Old Market offer freshly baked pretzels, making them a convenient treat for exploring the city.

## 9. Gelato at Eis-Greissler:

**Specialty**: Enjoy artisanal ice cream at Eis-Greissler with a variety of flavors made from local and organic ingredients.

**Location:** Located near Salzburg Cathedral, Eis-Greissler is the perfect place to refresh yourself and satisfy your sweet tooth.

Salzburg's street food scene offers a diverse and delicious selection of culinary delights combining traditional Austrian flavors with international influences. Whether you stroll the historic streets or explore the local markets, these 10 street food gems are a must-see for any tourist wanting to savor the vibrant and delicious side of Salzburg's food culture. Then set off on a culinary adventure and let your taste buds discover the rich array of flavors that Salzburg has to offer.

# Hidden Gems Beyond Tourist

# Paths

## St. Peter's Cemetery

Located in the heart of Salzburg, Austria, St. Peter's Cemetery is a testament to the city's rich history and cultural heritage. This centuries-old cemetery, with its ornate headstones and picturesque surroundings, offers visitors a unique glimpse into the past. Here you will find a comprehensive guide to help you make the most of your visit to St. Peter's Cemetery.

Founded in the 17th century, St. Peter's Cemetery is one of the oldest and most fascinating cemeteries in Austria. Its origins can be traced back to the Abbey of San Pietro, a Benedictine monastery founded in the 7th century. Over the centuries the cemetery has been the final resting place of both monks and citizens of Salzburg, creating a fascinating tapestry of stories and stories.

St. Peter's Cemetery is located at the foot of the Festungsberg, conveniently located in Salzburg's Altstadt (old town). The cemetery is easily accessible on foot, just a short walk from the famous Getreidegasse and the Hohensalzburg Fortress.

St. Peter's Cemetery is known for its Baroque and Rococo architecture, evident in the design of the gravestones and mausoleums. The cemetery is a serene oasis, surrounded by lush vegetation and decorated with fragrant flowers. The atmosphere exudes calm and offers a quiet retreat from the hustle and bustle of Salzburg.

The cemetery is home to a number of notable tombs and tombs, including that of Mozart's sister, Nannerl Mozart. Visitors can also find the grave of Haydn's younger brother, Michael Haydn, who was an important composer himself. The artfully and painstakingly designed tombs illustrate the artistic and cultural significance of the people buried here.

Next to the cemetery are the Catacombs of St. Peter, a fascinating network of burial chambers carved into the fortress mountain. These catacombs from the early Christian period offer a unique insight into the religious history of Salzburg. Guided tours are available allowing visitors to explore the eerie and fascinating underground chambers.

Saint-Pierre cemetery is generally open to the public all year round. However, it is advisable to check the exact opening times before planning your visit, as they may vary depending on the season and specific events. Take a guided tour to learn about the history and significance of the cemetery. Knowledgeable guides can provide insight into the stories behind the headstones and the cultural context of the site. The cemetery's unique architecture and picturesque setting make it a popular location for photography. Respect the solemn atmosphere and avoid disturbing other visitors while capturing the beauty of the site. Some tickets may offer combined access to St. Peter's Cemetery and the Catacombs of St. Peter. Check out special offers that allow you to explore both attractions at a discounted rate. St. Peter's Cemetery in Salzburg is much more than just a burial site; It is a living testimony to the city's rich cultural and artistic heritage. With its historic tombs, stunning architecture and tranquil atmosphere, a visit to St. Peter's Cemetery is a must for any traveler exploring the charming city of Salzburg. Take the time to appreciate the beauty and significance of this centuries-old site and you will immerse yourself in the captivating stories that resonate within the sacred places.

## Kapuzinerberg Hill

Located in the heart of Salzburg, Austria, Kapuzinerberg is a testament to the city's rich history and natural beauty. Named after the Capuchin monks who once lived in the area, this lush green oasis offers a peaceful escape from the hustle and bustle of the city. Whether you're a nature lover, history buff, or simply looking for panoramic views of Salzburg, Kapuzinerberg is a must-see for any traveler.

The origins of the Montagne des Capuchins date back to the 17th century, when Archbishop Paris Lodron had a monastery built for the Capuchin monks. Although the monastery no longer exists, the remains of the Capuchin complex, including the emblematic Capuchin Tower, still adorn the hill. The region has witnessed centuries of cultural development and its historical significance adds depth to the natural beauty that defines Kapuzinerberg today.

The Kapuzinerberg is a paradise for nature lovers. A network of well-marked hiking trails winds through the lush landscape, leading visitors to picturesque viewpoints and secluded places to relax.

The hill's diverse flora, including conifers and deciduous trees, creates a vibrant play of colors throughout the seasons. Spring brings blooming wildflowers, while fall dresses the hills in a fascinating array of reds and golds. Several well-developed hiking trails cater to different fitness levels and make the Kapuzinerberg accessible to everyone. The popular City View Trail offers stunning views of the Salzburg skyline, while the Woodland Path immerses hikers in the tranquility of the surrounding forest. For a more challenging climb, the Monastery Trail leads to where the Capuchin Monastery once stood, offering a glimpse into the area's historical roots.

One of the main attractions of the Kapuzinerberg is its incomparable panoramic views. From various vantage points, visitors can admire Salzburg's medieval and baroque architecture, including the iconic Hohensalzburg Fortress and the Salzach River as it winds through the city. Sunset is a particularly magical time to be on the hill, as the dying light casts a warm glow over the landscape.

The Capuchin Tower, an iconic monument on the Kapuzinerberg, offers visitors an elevated perspective of Salzburg. While the tower itself is not open to the public, the surrounding area offers a peaceful place to reflect and enjoy breathtaking views.

The Kapuzinerberg is located in the center of Salzburg and is easily accessible from the historic center. The hill can be reached on foot or via the Monchsberg lift, which connects the historic center with the Monchsberg plateau, of which the Kapuzinerberg is part. The trails are generally open year-round, but it's a good idea to check local conditions, especially in winter. Wear comfortable walking shoes, especially if you plan to explore hiking trails. Don't forget to bring water and sunscreen, especially in the warmer months.

The Kapuzinerberg is a peaceful retreat and offers a perfect blend of history and natural beauty. Whether you are an avid hiker or simply looking for a peaceful retreat, this Salzburg gem promises an unforgettable experience for every visitor.

## Augustiner Bräu Beer Garden

Located in the heart of Salzburg, the Augustiner Bräu beer garden is a testament to centuries-old brewing traditions and a hub for community celebrations. This iconic beer garden is not only a place to enjoy great beer, but also a cultural experience that immerses visitors in the rich history and friendliness of Salzburg.

The Augustiner Bräu Biergarten is located Lindhofstraße 7, 5020 Salzburg and is conveniently located close to the city center, making it easy to access for locals and tourists alike. The expansive beer garden offers guests plenty of space to enjoy the open-air atmosphere.

Augustiner Bräu was founded in 1621 and has a long and eventful history. Originally founded as a monastery brewery by Augustinian monks, it has become one of Austria's oldest and most beloved breweries. The beer garden, whose roots date back to the 19th century, has become an integral part of Salzburg's cultural identity.

Upon entering the beer garden, visitors are greeted by a unique blend of rustic charm and coziness. The large outdoor seating area is decorated with long wooden tables and benches, creating a communal atmosphere that encourages social interaction. Tall chestnut trees provide ample shade, making it an ideal place to relax and enjoy the company of friends or make new acquaintances. The highlight of any visit to Augustiner Bräu is undoubtedly the beer. The beer is served in traditional stone mugs and tapped directly from wooden barrels in the historic barrel cellar. The brewery produces a variety of beers, including the renowned Märzen, a malty, full-bodied lager. Visitors can also discover seasonal and specialty beers, each crafted with precision and according to the brewery's time-honored recipes.

To complement the exceptional beer selection, a wide range of traditional Austrian dishes are available at the food stands. From chewy pretzels to juicy roast pork, the menu caters to a variety of tastes. Visitors can taste local specialties while enjoying the lively atmosphere of the beer garden.

Augustiner Bräu is not just a place to enjoy beer and food; it is a cultural institution that promotes a sense of community. Locals and tourists mingle at long communal tables, creating an environment where strangers become friends amid laughter and clinking of glasses. This sense of community accurately reflects Austrian gemütlichkeit, a term that embodies warmth, friendliness and a sense of belonging. Augustiner Bräu hosts various events throughout the year, adding an extra level of excitement to the beer garden experience. Live music, traditional folk performances and seasonal festivals enhance the festive atmosphere and offer visitors the opportunity to take part in the local culture.

The beer garden is generally open daily, with longer opening hours on weekends and special events. We recommend that you consult the official website for the most up-to-date information. The preferred payment method is cash, although some kiosks also accept cards. Finding a seat at peak times can be a challenge, but sharing tables is part of the experience. Arriving early or outside peak hours can increase your chances of getting a place.

The Augustiner Bräu beer garden is not only a meeting point for beer lovers; It is a cultural pilgrimage for those seeking an authentic Austrian experience. With its rich history, friendly atmosphere and exceptional beer selection, this iconic beer garden remains a must-see for anyone exploring the charming city of Salzburg. Immerse yourself in centuries-old traditions, savor the flavors of Austrian cuisine and enjoy the vibrant community spirit that makes Augustiner Bräu a treasured gem in the heart of Salzburg.

# Shopping in Salzburg

## Old Town Boutiques

Nestled among Salzburg's charming streets and historic architecture lies a shopping paradise that captures the essence of the city's rich cultural heritage: the boutiques of the Old Town. This guide will take you on a comprehensive tour of these unique shops, ensuring you get the most out of your shopping experience as you immerse yourself in the beauty of Salzburg.

Old Town boutiques are scattered throughout Salzburg's Altstadt (Old Town), making them easily accessible to tourists exploring this UNESCO World Heritage site. The cobbled streets and baroque architecture create a picturesque backdrop and enhance the overall shopping experience. The boutiques are located in the immediate vicinity of emblematic places such as the Mirabell Palace, Mozart's birthplace and the Salzburg Cathedral. The boutiques in Salzburg's historic center are known for their distinctive offerings, ranging from traditional Austrian craftsmanship to modern, cutting-edge design. Here are some notable boutiques worth exploring:

**Getreidegasse:** This historic shopping street is known for its wrought-iron guild signs and is home to a variety of boutiques selling local fashion, jewelry, and souvenirs.

**Elsbethen-Gasse:** A charming street adorned with boutiques selling handmade goods, including leather goods, textiles and ceramics.

**Traditional Austrian crafts:**

Immerse yourself in Salzburg's rich cultural tapestry by exploring boutiques specializing in traditional **Austrian crafts. Beware of:**

Dirndl and Lederhosen Shops: These shops offer iconic traditional Austrian clothing, allowing tourists to take home a piece of authentic Austrian culture. Artisan Souvenirs: Artisan shops offer locally made souvenirs such as wood carvings, crystal glassware and artisan chocolate.

**Fashion and design stores:**

For those who prefer contemporary styles and innovative designs, the shops in Salzburg's Old Town cater to different tastes. Explore:

**Designer Fashion Shops**: Discover high-quality clothing from local and international designers, featuring unique pieces that reflect current trends.

**Art Galleries and Concept Stores:** Experience the fusion of art and fashion in concept stores that feature innovative designs and curated collections.

**Culinary delights:**

The shops in the Old Town are not limited to fashion and crafts. Indulge your taste buds by visiting gourmet boutiques offering:

**Local delicacies**: Discover shops selling regional delicacies including Mozartkugeln (Mozart chocolates), local cheeses and fine Austrian wines.

Specialty tea and coffee shops: Sample the flavors of Salzburg with a visit to tea and coffee boutiques, where you can find unique blends and locally roasted beans.

Most boutiques in Salzburg's Old Town are open from 10am to 6pm, with some variations. Please check specific store hours in advance. Make sure you have both cash and credit cards with you, as some smaller boutiques prefer cash transactions. Respect the local culture and ask permission before taking photos in shops.

The shops in Salzburg's Old Town offer an attractive mix of tradition and modernity and make shopping in the historic city a unique experience. Whether you're looking for traditional Austrian crafts, modern fashion, or delicious local treats, the shops of the Old Town have something to offer every visitor. Take your time, wander the enchanting streets and let Salzburg's shopping treasures become treasured memories of your travel adventure.

## Traditional Markets

Salzburg, the picturesque Austrian city located in the heart of the Alps, is known not only for its stunning architecture and musical heritage, but also for its lively traditional markets. These markets offer a delicious mix of local flavours, crafts and cultural experiences, making them an essential part of any Salzburg itinerary. In this comprehensive travel guide we take you on a journey through Salzburg's traditional markets and provide you with all the information you need to get the most out of your visit.

**Know the markets:**

Salzburg offers a variety of traditional markets throughout the year, each with its own unique charm. The most famous markets are the Green Market (Grünmarkt), the Christmas Market (Christkindlmarkt) and the Easter Market (Ostermarkt). These markets are not only excellent places for shopping, but also offer cultural immersion in the heart of Salzburg.

**Green Market (Grünmarkt):**

*Location: University Square (Universitätsplatz)*

When: Open all year, from Monday to Saturday

What to expect: Fresh produce, local delicacies, handmade crafts and a lively atmosphere. The green market is a foodie's paradise, with stalls selling fresh fruit, vegetables, cheeses, meat and sweets. It is the perfect place to enjoy the authentic taste of Salzburg.

**Christmas Market (Christkindlmarkt):**

*Location: Residenzplein (Residenzplatz) and Cathedral Square (Domplatz)*

When: from the end of November to December

What to expect: The enchanting Christkindlmarkt transforms Salzburg into a winter wonderland. Explore wooden stalls adorned with festive decorations, enjoy seasonal treats such as roasted chestnuts and mulled wine, and discover handmade jewelery and gifts. The market is a magical experience for visitors of all ages.

**Easter Market (Ostermarkt):**

*Location: Residenzplein (Residenzplatz)*

When: from the end of March to April

What to expect: Celebrate the arrival of spring at the Ostermarkt, where you'll find intricately decorated Easter eggs, traditional Austrian craftsmanship and a cheerful atmosphere. Enjoy local culinary delights and take part in Easter celebrations that reflect the spirit of the season.

**Local cuisine and delicacies:**

Don't miss the chance to taste local specialties such as Mozartkugel (Mozart balls), Sacher Torte (chocolate cake) and Salzburg Nockerl (a sweet soufflé). The markets offer a wide range of street food, from traditional sausages to hearty stews and pretzels. It's a great way to experience the authentic flavors of Salzburg.

**Cultural experiences:**

Many markets offer live music, traditional dance performances and cultural events. Consult the program to immerse yourself in local arts and traditions.

**Practical advice for visitors:**

Take into account market times and seasonal variations. Bring cash for small purchases as some merchants may not accept cards.

Dress warmly for the winter markets, as the Alpine climate in Salzburg can be chilly.

In short, Salzburg's traditional markets are not just places to go shopping; they are living expressions of the city's rich cultural heritage. From the lively Green Market to the festive Christmas and Easter markets, these activity centers are essential stops for any traveler wanting to experience the authentic atmosphere of Salzburg. So put on your walking shoes, embrace the festive atmosphere and travel through the traditional markets that make Salzburg truly unique.

## Unique Souvenirs

As you explore the charming streets of Salzburg, you'll take home more than just souvenirs: immerse yourself in the local culture and discover unique souvenirs that reflect the city's heritage. In this comprehensive guide, we'll show you the best tips for buying unique souvenirs in Salzburg.

**Traditional clothing and accessories:**

Dirndl and Lederhosen: Immerse yourself in Austrian tradition by investing in traditional clothing. Dirndls for women and lederhosen for men are not only trendy, but also represent the rich cultural heritage of Salzburg.

**Traditional Costume Accessories:** Complement your clothing with finely crafted traditional costume accessories, such as hats, belts and jewelry, and showcase the craftsmanship and style of the region. Mozart themed memories:

**Mozartkugeln (Mozart Balls):** No trip to Salzburg is complete without enjoying Mozartkugeln, chocolate balls filled with marzipan and nougat, a tribute to the city's most famous musical son, Wolfgang Amadeus Mozart.

Mozart memorabilia: Discover several shops offering Mozart-themed souvenirs, such as music boxes, key chains and figurines, which will add a musical touch to your souvenirs.

**Handmade Christmas decorations:**

Salzburg is known for its Christmas traditions and you can bring some of the festive charm home with handmade Christmas decorations. These unique decorations often feature intricate details and are perfect for commemorating your visit during the holidays.

**Salzburg salt and salt products:**

Salzburg Mozartkugeln: not to be confused with chocolate Mozartkugeln, these are salt balls produced from the Salzburg salt mines. They come in a variety of flavors and make a unique culinary souvenir.

Salt-based beauty products: Explore local stores for skin care products made with Salzburg salt, known for its therapeutic properties. From bath salts to skin care creams, these items make thoughtful yet practical gifts.

**Hand Painted Easter Eggs:**

Easter is celebrated with great enthusiasm in Salzburg and hand-painted eggs are a popular tradition. Look for beautifully designed Easter eggs with intricate patterns and vibrant colors that capture the spirit of the season. Local arts and crafts:

**Visit the Old Town Galleries**: Explore the narrow streets of Salzburg's Old Town and discover local art galleries. Purchase paintings, sculptures or crafts that reflect the creativity of the region's artists.

**Traditional woodworking:** Look for wooden crafts, including toys, tools and decorative objects, that demonstrate the region's dedication to traditional craftsmanship.

**Austrian liqueurs and grappas:**

Local liqueurs: Enjoy the flavors of Salzburg by bringing home locally produced liqueurs and schnapps. Look for bottles with unique labels or flavors that highlight the region's diverse distilling traditions. Salzburg offers a delightful selection of unique souvenirs that stand out from the ordinary and allow you to take home a piece of its rich culture and history. From traditional clothing and

97

Mozart-themed items to handcrafted ornaments and local art, each souvenir tells a story about the city's living heritage. As you explore the enchanting streets, don't forget to bring these precious souvenirs with you to make your visit to Salzburg truly unforgettable.

# Day Trips from Salzburg

## The Lakes District

Nestled in the enchanting landscape of Salzburg, Austria is the Lake District, a fascinating region that perfectly combines natural beauty and cultural richness. This guide aims to give tourists a comprehensive overview of the Lake District, providing information on its picturesque lakes, charming villages and countless activities that await those seeking an unforgettable experience in this idyllic corner of the world.

The lake area is located in the Salzkammergut and is easily accessible from the center of Salzburg. Tourists can reach the lake district by car, train or bus and enjoy scenic routes showcasing the beautiful Austrian countryside. Driving is an integral part of the experience and every turn reveals lush vegetation, alpine meadows and pristine lakes. The Lake District is known for its crystal clear lakes, each with its own unique charm. Wolfgangsee, Fuschlsee and Mondsee are the crown jewels, surrounded by majestic mountains and adorned with historic lakeside villages. Visitors can take boat trips, swim in crystal clear waters or simply relax on the coast while admiring breathtaking scenery.

Exploring the Lake District is not complete without immersing yourself in the charm of the lakeside villages. St. Gilgen, St. Wolfgang and Mondsee are among the most picturesque, offering cobbled streets, colorful houses and historic architecture.

Stroll through these charming villages and discover local cafes, boutiques and cultural treasures.

The Lake District is rich in history and culture. Mondsee, for example, is home to the famous Mondsee Monastery, where the wedding scene from "The Sound of Music" was filmed. St. Wolfgang is home to the St. Wolfgang Pilgrimage Church, a masterpiece of Gothic architecture. Furthermore, Falkenstein Castle offers a glimpse into medieval life and panoramic views of the surrounding landscape. Nature lovers and adventure seekers will find plenty of activities to enjoy. Hiking trails wind through the hills and offer stunning views of the surrounding lakes and mountains. Water sports such as sailing, kayaking and boating are popular on the lakes and offer an exciting way to experience the crystal clear waters. Cyclists can explore scenic routes around the lakes and enjoy the fresh mountain air and breathtaking scenery.

The Lake District is a foodie's paradise and offers a delicious range of Austrian dishes. Lakeside restaurants serve fresh fish, local cheese and traditional Austrian desserts. Visitors can taste regional specialties while admiring panoramic views of lakes and mountains.

Throughout the year, the Lakes region hosts numerous festivals and events celebrating local traditions, music and art. The St. Wolfgang Advent market in winter and the St. Gilgen festival in summer are just a few examples of the region's vibrant cultural life.

The Lakes Region is a year-round destination and each season offers a unique experience. Summer is ideal for outdoor activities, while winter transforms the region into a snowy wonderland.

Renting a car offers flexibility, but public transportation options are available for those who prefer not to drive.

Lakeside hotels, charming guesthouses and cozy bed and breakfasts offer a range of accommodation options to suit different preferences and budgets.

The Salzburg Lake District is a treasure trove of natural beauty, cultural heritage and outdoor adventures. Whether you're looking for relaxation, cultural immersion or adrenaline-pumping

103

activities, this enchanting region has something to offer every traveler. Immerse yourself in the timeless charm of the Lake District, where landscapes tell stories and every moment is a perfect memory waiting to be captured.

## Eisriesenwelt Ice Caves

Nestled in the magnificent inwerfen of the Tennengebirge, a short drive south of Salzburg, the Eisriesenwelt is considered one of Austria's most breathtaking natural wonders. With a history dating back to their discovery in 1879, these caves have captured the imagination of travelers around the world. Whether you are an adventurer or a nature lover, a visit to the Eisriesenwelt promises an unforgettable experience. This comprehensive guide provides all the essential information you need to get the most out of your visit to this fascinating ice cave system.

The Eisriesenwelt is easily accessible from Salzburg. A scenic 40-minute drive takes you through the picturesque Salzach Valley to the town of Werden. From there, a short bus or taxi ride will take you to the base of the mountain, where the adventure really begins. It's a good idea to check opening times and weather conditions before planning your trip, as the caves are only accessible during the warmer months, usually May to October.

In order to explore the world of the ice giants, visitors must take a guided tour. Available in a variety of languages, these tours provide insightful commentary on the cave's history, geology, and fascinating formations. Tickets can be purchased at the visitor center or online. It is recommended to book in advance, especially in high tourist season. Prepare for a moderate hike to reach the cave entrance. So wear comfortable shoes and dress for the weather.

The Eisriesenwelt stretches for 42 kilometers, making it the largest ice cave system in the world. However, only a small part of the caves, approximately 1 kilometer, is open to the public. The tour lasts approximately 75 minutes and includes both the large ice rinks and the intricate ice formations such as stalactites and stalagmites, which are illuminated to enhance their magical appeal. The temperature in the caves is around freezing. Make sure to bring warm clothes with you, even during the summer months.

The enchanting beauty of the world of ice giants is a dream for any photographer. Don't forget to bring a camera with a low-light feature to capture the ethereal glow of the ice formations. Tripods are not allowed in the caves. Therefore, for best results, you should use a high ISO setting and a wide aperture. Don't forget to charge your camera or bring spare batteries, as cold temperatures can drain the battery faster than usual. In order to protect the sensitive environment of the Eisriesenwelt, visitors are required to follow certain guidelines. Touching the ice formations is strictly prohibited and visitors are asked to stay on designated trails. Additionally, food and drinks are not allowed in the caves. Respect for nature ensures that future generations will also be able to marvel at the wonders of the ice giant world.

A visit to the Eisriesenwelt is a journey into an underground world of incomparable beauty. From the majestic ice formations to the rich history of their discoveries, these caves offer an experience that will remain etched in your memory. When planning your trip to Salzburg, be sure to include the Eisriesenwelt in your itinerary for a truly magical and unforgettable adventure.

## Hallstatt: A UNESCO World Heritage Site

Nestled in the breathtaking landscapes of the Austrian Alps, Hallstatt is a picturesque jewel in the Salzburg region. Recognized as a UNESCO World Heritage Site, this charming village offers a captivating mix of natural beauty, rich history and cultural significance. When you embark on your trip to Salzburg, be sure to include Hallstatt in your itinerary for an unforgettable experience.

Located approximately 73 kilometers from the city of Salzburg, reaching Hallstatt is an enchanting journey in itself. The scenic drive or train journey through the Austrian countryside offers a glimpse of the breathtaking landscapes that await you in this mountain paradise. Alternatively, you can also take a boat trip on Lake Hallstatt for a unique approach to the village.

Hallstatt is known for its idyllic location, nestled between the Dachstein Alps and the pristine Hallstätter See (Lake Hallstatt). The village is surrounded by towering mountains and offers perfect views that change with the seasons. Whether it's the snow-capped peaks in winter or the lush greenery in summer, Hallstatt's natural beauty is a sight to behold.

With a history dating back to prehistoric times, Hallstatt is a treasure chest of cultural treasures. Explore the Hallstatt-Dachstein/Salzkammergut cultural landscape, which highlights the village's prehistoric origins, its rich salt mining history, and the unique burial customs of the Hallstatt period. Visit the Hallstatt Museum to delve deeper into the region's past and discover archaeological artifacts that reveal the ancient roots of this charming village.

**Main attractions:**

**Hallstatt Skywalk:** For a panoramic view of the village and surrounding mountains, take a ride on the Hallstatt Skywalk. Situated on an elevated platform, the Skywalk offers a breathtaking vantage point to capture the beauty of Hallstatt.

**Dachstein Ice Cave**: A short drive away is the Dachstein Ice Cave, a fascinating natural wonder. Explore underground ice formations and marvel at the breathtaking crystalline structures that have formed over centuries.

**Hallstatt Salt Mine**: Learn about the history of salt mining in Hallstatt with a visit to the Hallstatt Salt Mine. Take a guided tour in the heart of the mountains and discover the importance of salt for the economic and cultural development of the region.

**Market Square**: Stroll through the heart of Hallstatt and enjoy the charm of the Market Square. Admire pastel-colored buildings, visit local shops, and enjoy traditional Austrian cuisine in quaint cafes. Lake Hallstatt Boat Tour: Explore the crystal clear waters of Lake Hallstatt on a boat tour. Admire the reflections of the surrounding mountains on the surface of the lake and enjoy the tranquility of this alpine paradise.

Although Hallstatt is charming all year round, consider visiting in late spring or early fall, when the weather is milder and there are fewer crowds. Plan your trip in advance, whether by car, train or boat, and check timetables to optimize your travel time. Book your accommodation in advance as Hallstatt is a popular travel destination and accommodation options can fill up quickly. Don't miss the opportunity to enjoy traditional Austrian dishes in local restaurants. Try regional specialties such as Wiener Schnitzel and Sachertorte. Hallstatt is a small village, so please be respectful of local residents and comply with any guidelines or regulations to maintain the tranquility of the area.

In conclusion, a visit to Hallstatt promises an immersive experience in the heart of Austria's natural and cultural heritage. From breathtaking landscapes to rich history, this UNESCO World Heritage site offers a perfect mix of relaxation and discovery for every traveler. Make Hallstatt an essential part of your trip to Salzburg for an authentic Austrian adventure.

## Wellness and Relaxation

Salzburg not only offers a rich cultural experience, but also a paradise for lovers of wellness and relaxation. Whether you seek relaxation in thermal baths, peace in yoga retreats or want to be pampered in the tranquil atmosphere of Alpine wellness resorts, Salzburg has it all. Let's explore in detail what the city has to offer those who want to relax and prioritize their well-being.

Salzburg has a number of world-class spa resorts that offer a perfect blend of luxury and therapeutic benefits. An exceptional excursion destination is the Felsentherme in the picturesque Gastein Valley. Imagine enjoying geothermal water surrounded by the beautiful Austrian Alps. Felsentherme Spa offers a range of wellness services, from invigorating saunas to relaxing massages, ensuring visitors have a holistic experience.

For those seeking a more intimate setting, the Rupertus Therme in Bad Reichenhall offers a unique blend of traditional and modern spa facilities. The spas here are fed by ancient Alpine salt deposits, known for their healing properties. Visitors can enjoy saltwater pools, saunas and exclusive spa treatments, offering a serene escape from the hustle and bustle of everyday life. Salzburg's tranquil landscapes and tranquil atmosphere make it an ideal destination for yoga enthusiasts seeking inner peace. The city offers various yoga retreats aimed at people of all levels, from beginner to advanced.

A remarkable hideaway can be found on the outskirts of Salzburg, surrounded by lush greenery and the calming sounds of nature. Participants can participate in daily yoga sessions led by experienced teachers, meditate in tranquil gardens, and enjoy nutritious meals using local produce. The retreat offers an ideal opportunity to disconnect from the digital world and reconnect with yourself in a peaceful and relaxing environment. For those who want a wellness experience in breathtaking Alpine scenery, Salzburg's Alpine wellness resorts offer the perfect combination of luxury and nature. These resorts are designed to offer guests an immersive experience, combining the healing power of nature with modern comforts.

One such resort, located on the slopes of the Austrian Alps, offers panoramic views of the surrounding mountains. During the day you can enjoy outdoor activities, such as hiking and skiing, and in the evening, relax in the resort's state-of-the-art spa facilities. From outdoor hot tubs overlooking snow-capped peaks to specialized Alpine-inspired spa treatments, these resorts are redefining relaxation in a truly Austrian way. Salzburg, with its thermal baths, yoga retreats and Alpine wellness resorts, is known as a holistic wellness destination. Visitors can expect to rejuvenate their mind, body and soul amidst the beautiful natural landscapes and cultural richness the city has to offer. Whether you are seeking the therapeutic benefits of thermal waters, the tranquility of yoga retreats or the luxury of wellness in the Alps, Salzburg offers a wellness experience that transcends the ordinary. Embrace

tranquility, enjoy self-care and let Salzburg be your

guide to holistic well-being.

# Currency and Banking

The official currency of Austria and therefore of Salzburg is the euro (€). Euros are available in denominations of 5, 10, 20, 50, 100, 200 and 500 euros. Euro coins are available in denominations of 1, 2, 5, 10, 20 and 50 centimes as well as 1 and 2 euros.

There are a number of banks in Salzburg, including international and Austrian banks. The largest banks in Salzburg include:

- Erste Bank

- Raiffeisenbank

- Bank Austria

- Hypo Tirol Bank

- Volksbank Salzburg

119

Most banks in Salzburg are open Monday to Friday from 8:00 a.m. to 4:00 p.m. Some banks are also open on Saturdays from 9:00 to 13:00.

In Salzburg there are numerous ATMs, both in bank branches and in public places such as shopping centers and train stations. ATMs in Salzburg accept most major international debit and credit cards. In Salzburg there are several exchange offices where you can exchange foreign currencies for euros. Exchange offices are located in banks, train stations and tourist offices. It's always a good idea to have a few euros with you when traveling to Salzburg, as not all stores accept foreign currency. You can withdraw euros from Salzburg ATMs with your foreign debit or credit card. However, you may be charged a fee for this service. If you are exchanging a large amount of foreign currencies, you should compare the exchange rates of different exchange offices before making your decision. Tipping is not expected in Austria, but it is welcome. For good service it is customary to leave a small tip of 10%. Always make sure to keep your money and valuables safe. Never leave your money unattended. Be aware of your surroundings and use caution when withdrawing money from ATMs. If you lose your money or credit card, contact your bank or card issuer immediately.

# Useful Websites and Apps

To make the most of your visit, here is a comprehensive guide to useful websites and apps for your trip to Salzburg:

**1. Salzburg official tourism website:**

Tourism in Salzburg: The official tourism website provides extensive information on attractions, events, accommodation and practical advice. You can find maps, suggested routes and details about the Salzburg Card, which offers discounts on various attractions.

**2. Google Maps:**

Google Maps: An essential tool for navigating, finding local businesses, and planning your routes.

Make sure to download offline maps for Salzburg to navigate without using data.

**3. Salzburg Map Application:**

Salzburg Card App: If you decide to purchase the Salzburg Card to benefit from discounted entry to museums and public transport, this app will inform you about the included attractions and help you plan your itinerary.

**4. TripAdvisor:**

TripAdvisor: Read reviews and recommendations from other travelers for attractions, restaurants, and accommodations. This can be a valuable resource for making informed decisions during your trip.

## 5. Weather Apps:

Weather.com or your favorite weather app: Keep an eye on the weather forecast to plan your outdoor activities and pack accordingly.

## 6. Uber or Mytaxi:

Uber or Mytaxi: for convenient and reliable transportation around town, especially if you're unfamiliar with public transportation. 7. Cultural trip:

Cultural Tour: Discover hidden gems, local events, and unique experiences recommended by locals. It's a great app for exploring off-the-beaten-path sites.

**8. WiFi Search:**

WiFi finder apps: Find free WiFi hotspots around Salzburg to stay connected without excessive roaming charges.

**9. Duolingo or Google Translate:**

Duolingo or Google Translate: Although many locals speak English, a basic knowledge of German can be helpful. These apps can help with translation if necessary.

**10. Eventbrite or Meetup:**

Eventbrite or Meetup: Find out about local events, concerts and meetups happening during your visit to immerse yourself in the city's cultural scene.

## 11. Public Transportation Apps:

**ÖBB Scotty:** If you plan to explore beyond Salzburg, this app from the Austrian Federal Railways will help you find train times.

**Salzburg Verkehrs app:** information about buses and local transport in Salzburg.

## 12. Currency Converter Apps:

XE Currency Converter: Keep an eye on exchange rates to manage your spending efficiently.

## 13. WhatsApp or Viber:

WhatsApp or Viber: Stay in touch with friends, family and travel companions via messaging and voice calls over Wi-Fi.

### 14. Instagram or Pinterest:

Instagram or Pinterest: Explore visual content for travel inspiration and use location tags to discover popular places and hidden gems.

Don't forget to check the latest app reviews and updates before you travel, as technology and services may evolve. With these tools you will be well equipped to explore Salzburg and get the most out of your travel experience.

# Emergency Contacts

EU Emergency Number: 112 (free from any phone)

Fire Brigade: 122

Police: 133

Doctors' Emergency Service: 141

Ambulance Service: 144

ÖAMTC: 120

ARBÖ: 123

Crisis Hotline: 142

Emergency Services for Children and Young People: 147

Salzburg Tourist Information: +43 662 88989-0

When calling an emergency number from your cell phone, it is important to first dial the area code (0662 for Salzburg) and then the emergency number. If you don't speak German, you can ask the operator to put you in touch with an English-speaking provider. In an emergency, it is important to remain calm and provide as much information as possible to the operator. This includes your location, the type of emergency, and the number of people involved. It's a good idea to carry a list of emergency contacts when you travel. You can also download the Austrian Red Cross "Notfall App". This app provides access to emergency numbers, first aid instructions and a list of hospitals and pharmacies. If you are staying in a hotel, ask the

front desk for a list of emergency contacts. Make
sure you have travel insurance that covers medical
emergencies.

# Conclusion

At the end of your trip to Salzburg, take a moment to reflect on the rich array of experiences this enchanting city has woven for you. Salzburg, with its breathtaking mountain landscapes, historic architecture and cultural richness, has probably left an indelible mark on your heart.

During your stay here you may have explored the charming Old Town, strolled through the vibrant Mirabell Gardens or admired the breathtaking views from Hohensalzburg Fortress. Perhaps you've immersed yourself in the world of classical music, followed in Mozart's footsteps, or caught a show at the famous Salzburg Festival.

In addition to the tourist attractions, Salzburg's welcoming atmosphere and friendly people make you feel part of the community. Whether you're enjoying traditional Austrian cuisine at a local tavern or striking up lively conversations with locals, you've likely discovered the warmth and hospitality that define Salzburg.

As you reflect on your experience in Salzburg, think about the moments that remain most memorable for you. Maybe it was the sound of music echoing through the streets, the taste of a delicious Sachertorte or the breathtaking sunset over the Salzach. Either way, take these memories with you as treasured keepsakes and weave them into the fabric of your own life story.

Salzburg, with its timeless charm, creates memories that last long after you say goodbye. Ensuring that these moments are not only held in your heart, but also shared with others, is an essential part of the travel experience. Here are some tips for capturing and immortalizing your memories in Salzburg:

Equip yourself with a good camera or smartphone to capture the picturesque landscapes, architectural wonders and vibrant energy of the city streets. Create a visual diary of your trip to Salzburg, from the baroque splendor of Residenzplatz to the tranquility of Salzburg Cathedral.

Keep a travel diary to document your thoughts, feelings, and the nuances of your Salzburg adventure. Capture the details of each day, including the hidden gems you encountered, conversations with locals, and unexpected surprises that made your trip unique. Bring back a piece of Salzburg by collecting local souvenirs. Whether it's a traditional opera, a handmade Mozartkugel, or a unique work of art, these items serve as tangible reminders of your time spent in the city.

The people you meet can be the most memorable part of your trip. Document your interactions with locals, for example through interviews, photos or short videos, and showcase the authentic human stories that make Salzburg special.

By capturing your memories of Salzburg in various forms, you will not only create a lasting memory for yourself, but also contribute to the collective tapestry of travel knowledge. Whether as a personal keepsake or as an aid to future travelers, your experiences in Salzburg will become a treasured part of the city's continuing narrative.

Printed in Great Britain
by Amazon

42486648R00076